THE ZULU

A traditional Zulu homestead or *umuzi* (2) consists of a group of dwellings arranged in a circle, with the cattle byre in the centre. If possible, the homestead is built on a slope to provide drainage during the rainy season. The traditional house is beehive in shape and made almost entirely from natural materials. The men are responsible for building a framework of saplings. To this the women tie thatching grass, which is further secured by grass rope to prevent it from blowing loose in the wind (3).

The floor is made from hardened earth which is regularly smeared with cow dung to keep it clean and provide a glossy finish. Smoke from the hearth, which is situated in the centre, discourages insects from nesting in the thatch. Household utensils and other implements are hung from the roof and walls, while the rear area is used to store pots. This is also the place visited by the ancestral spirits and, to show that the family has not neglected its duties to them, the horns of cattle, which have been slaughtered as a sacrifice to the ancestors, are placed over the main doorway.

Traditional Zulu houses have no windows and only one doorway (1), which is low and rounded so that a person has to stoop in order to enter. An enemy of the family entering in this position is therefore at a disadvantage. At night the entrance is closed by a woven door made of wattle saplings, but, in spite of the thick thatch, the lack of windows and the low entrance, the houses are well ventilated. Smaller shelters, raised on stilts, are erected for storing grain.

An extended family live together in a homestead and houses are arranged in a set order, with the house of the head of the family being located roughly opposite the main entrance. As traditional Zulu society is polygynous, a man may have several wives, each of whom is entitled to her own house. The first wife of a commoner is the most senior and her house is the first one situated on the left-hand side of her husband, while the second wife occupies the first house on his right-hand side, and so on. Unmarried girls and boys have separate houses, located on either side of the main entrance.

3

4

The homestead is a self-sufficient unit: crops are cultivated by the women, while the cattle provide the family with milk and meat. However, today many items, such as soap, clothing, butter and salt, are purchased from the local store. As the cattle are a man's wealth and supply the bride wealth or *lobolo* for additional wives, they are given special protection, with the byre being situated in the centre of the *umuzi*, surrounded by the family's homes.

Although beehive houses still occur in the remoter areas of KwaZulu-Natal, it is not unusual to see a mix of traditional and modern houses in the same *umuzi*. Dwellings made from a framework of wattle branches and daub (4) with thatch or corrugated iron roofs, as well as western-style brick houses with brightly decorated walls, are now quite common.

5

6

Zulu society is patriarchal, and once a woman is married she leaves her father's homestead to go and live with her husband's family. The eldest son of a man's first wife usually assumes control of the homestead after his death.

Family members eat together at meal times, and the women and young girls are responsible for preparing the food for the household. Their daily meals are simple, consisting largely of maize, sweet potatoes, pumpkins, and sorghum eaten with curdled milk known as *amasi*. Maize is eaten either on the cob or it is ground and boiled in a three-legged cast iron pot to form a stiff porridge or *phuthu* (6). More elaborate meals, which would include meat, are cooked on special or ceremonial occasions.

The thick, grey beer made from ground sorghum, known as *umqombothi,* is brewed in a beer making hut filled with large baskets for storing the sorghum and pots which are used as vats during fermentation (7). The beer is strained through a long, cylindrical grass sieve which is twisted to remove all the liquid. Before the beer is tasted, the woman will skim off the scum that has formed on the top and put it on the ground next to the pot as an offering to the ancestral spirits. She tastes the beer and, if it is good, offers some to the head of the household (5) and then to everybody else present. The beer pot is covered with a grass lid which is sometimes decorated with beads. It is placed either in a downwards or upwards position, indicating whether the 'bar' is open or not.

7

8

Cattle are central to Zulu culture and the Nguni breed, in particular, are highly prized. Dealing with the livestock is a male activity (8), and young boys assist with milking the cattle and tending them while they are out grazing in the fields. Cattle are not only a measure of a man's wealth, but, without them, he would not be able to marry, as traditionally the *lobolo* is paid in cattle. However, these days payment is made in the cash equivalent. The cattle enclosure (9) is considered to be a sacred place of the ancestors and women are not permitted to enter, other than on special occasions.

A Zulu man has a spiritual rapport with his beasts – he knows them all by name and can plough a field by issuing verbal commands only.

It is considered rude to walk into a Zulu homestead without first asking permission, and therefore visitors customarily call out on approaching to announce their presence. Alternatively they will wait at the entrance until an adult member of the homestead notices them and invites them in. Often visitors have travelled long distances and so beer is offered, not only as a thirst quencher, but as part of accepted Zulu etiquette.

9

The life of a Zulu woman is one of hard, physical labour. She rears the children, collects the firewood and water (12), and cultivates the crops. The main crops which are grown consist of maize, sweet potatoes, pumpkins and sorghum. From sorghum women make a thick, grey beer known as *umqombothi*. This beverage forms an essential part of a Zulu man's diet and social interaction, and a woman who makes good beer is considered to be quite an asset.

It is not unusual for the wives of the same man to dress in a similar style, although it would not be proper for a junior wife to outdo the more senior wives. As a mark of respect to her husband and his family, a married woman must keep her breasts covered, therefore she traditionally wears a breast cover made from leather or cloth which is decorated with beads. When a woman is married she no longer dresses in the traditional short, beaded skirt and head-band worn by an unmarried girl (14), but changes her attire to a heavy, pleated skirt made from ox hide, and a large structured headdress constructed from knitting wool and clay (11 and 13).

The shape and size of a headdress indicate the age and status of the wearer as well as the area from which she hails (10). In the past these head-dresses were woven into the hair, but today they can be put on or removed like a hat. The women in the Msinga area of KwaZulu-Natal favour especially large circular headdresses which they cover with red ochre and then drape in brightly coloured fabric. Both married and unmarried women from this region tie colourful cloaks around their shoulders which, together with the beaded necklaces and leg bands, produce a striking effect.

12

13

14

15

16

17

18

19

20

21

Zulu people are renowned for their multi-hued beadwork, and at an early age young girls learn the use of various colour combinations and patterns to convey messages, usually about love and courtship (16). Zulu beadwork is used not only in necklaces, but is interwoven with grass and leather to make elaborate belts, aprons and skirts. It also decorates headdresses (19), calabashes and ceremonial sticks. In the past gut was used to string beads, but nowadays a needle and cotton are favoured (15 and 17). Occasionally antelope horns are included in the beadwork worn by Zulu men (20).

Although the finer distinctions of colour symbolism are not as readily understood as in the past, there are several broad categories which still apply. White generally means love, pink poverty, red passion and black adversity. Green could mean lush pastures or it could refer to a girl being as thin as a blade of grass because she has been separated from her man and is missing him. The amount of colour applied is also significant as it indicates the intensity of the emotion.

Before the advent of the early white settlers, beads were made from shells, wood and bone, and necklaces of olive wood were presented to Zulu warriors who showed great bravery in battle. The early traders introduced the Zulu to colourful glass beads, which were used to barter for skins and ivory, and so initiated the colour symbolism of Zulu beadwork. Today bright plastic beads are also used, especially in wide girdles and on the tasselled skirts worn by the young Zulu women at weddings and coming of age ceremonies (18 and 21).

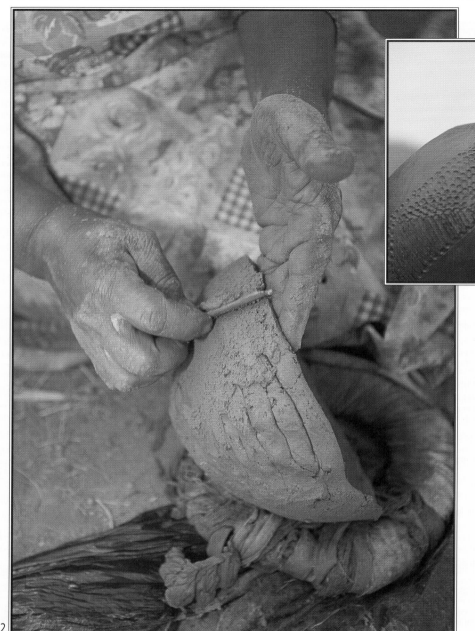

22

23

then smoothed out with a blade or stone (22). The shaped pot is baked in a fire made with aloe leaves to ensure a long, intense heat. After the pot has been fired it is a reddish-brown colour which is not considered ideal by the Zulu. For this reason it is covered in dry grass and burnt again, the smoke causing the outside to become black (24). The finished pot is rubbed down to give a glossy shine.

Traditional patterns on Zulu pottery are usually triangular, square and circular in shape and are made on the outside of the pot with a sharpened stick (23). Both the beer and water pots are fat-bellied and of similar shape (25), but the beer pot has no lip around the rim which makes drinking easier, as the beer is drunk either directly from the pot or scooped out with a calabash. The water pot, however, has a lip to prevent spillage, as the Zulu women use this pot to collect water and, like most heavy loads, carry the full pot on their heads. A ring of grass or cloth, known as *inkatha*, is sometimes placed on top of the head to cushion the weight of the pot and help steady it. Different sized pots have various uses around the home, but perhaps the most intriguing is the half-sized beer pot known as the 'stingy pot'. If a guest is offered beer from one of these pots, he knows that he is not very welcome and should not linger for too long.

Some adaptations in size and shape have been introduced in response to the tourist market, but the Zulu remain conservative as far as their pottery is concerned, preferring the traditional shapes and decorative patterns.

For centuries clay pottery has been made by the Zulu, whose women are expert potters. The shape and design of their pots have changed little over the years, and the quality of the end product is high. The consistency of the clay is important to a good potter and Zulu women will go to great lengths to obtain clay from the right source, often travelling a long way to find it.

Without the use of a pottery wheel they have nevertheless managed to create almost perfectly round pots by using the coil method. The dried clay is first ground into a fine powder and mixed with water before being rolled into long strips and wound around into the desired shape of the pot required. The sides are

24

25

26

27

28

29

30

Both Zulu men and women are skilled craft makers, each using different mediums to express their talents. The items made are not only for personal use and adornment but also for use around the home and for sale to the growing number of tourists appreciative of the various Zulu art forms.

In addition to their beadwork and pottery, Zulu women are excellent weavers (26). From grass and palm leaves they are able to fashion a wide variety of articles which include grain storage baskets, beer strainers, plaited bangles, leg bands, mats, bags, belts and bowls (29). Certain bowls are so tightly woven that they are able to hold liquids. Grasses dyed in different colours are used in baskets (27), and patterns made from knitting wool are woven into the highly prized bridal mats which are created out of a very fine grass known as *ncema* grass (30).

Zulu basketware is particularly popular with the tourists and traditional articles have been adapted to suit this market. Brightly coloured shopping baskets, pot plant holders and table mats are examples of this adaptation (28), but perhaps the most interesting is the use of the traditional Zulu sleeping mat as something to sit or tan on while at the beach.

The men, who are renowned for their wood carvings, use small knives and choppers to produce spoons, bowls, meat trays, ceremonial sticks and spear handles. Household utensils are further decorated by charring patterns into the wood. Excellent carvings of wild animals and birds are also skilfully charred and painted with dyes to sell to the tourists.

31

32

From an early age Zulu children are taught to respect their elders and to assist around the homestead wherever possible. The chores are divided along traditional lines, the girls helping their mothers with the cooking and collecting of firewood and water, while the boys tend to the cattle and goats. As Zulu women transport heavy loads on their heads, often over long distances, the young girls soon learn how to balance pots of water or bundles of wood on theirs (32). The girls are further expected to look after their younger sisters and brothers, and it is not unusual to see a young girl, even as little as six years old, carrying a baby on her back.

Acceptable behaviour and good manners are endorsed during mealtimes, which are leisurely family affairs. Like all children, Zulu children learn by example and in this way the skills of wood carving and spear and shield making are passed on to the

boys, and the art of beadwork, pottery and weaving to the girls. Dancing, singing and music are an integral part of Zulu culture and exposure to these traditions ensures that the children take pride in their heritage. They learn about Zulu history and customs through the medium of story-telling. This oral tradition still endures today, in spite of the children attending school and being able to read about their culture.

Since a Zulu man may have several wives and thus many children (34), traditional family groups are large and chores are shared between a number of siblings, allowing time to play (33). Early responsibilities make Zulu children independent and resourceful. They use stones and bottle caps to play games and the boys make their own intricate car toys out of wire, complete with workable steering. Stick fighting is a great sport among the boys and in their free time they will spend hours competing against one another. Even very young boys have their own sticks and know the rules, different techniques and body positions of the sport. Living in rural KwaZulu-Natal, the children grow up playing in the fields and rivers (31) where they learn to throw their hunting sticks or clubs to stun small animals and to catch fish for the pot.

Besides their more traditional pursuits, Zulu boys are also avid soccer players and most communities have soccer fields, even in the remotest areas. Competitions between opposing sides are keenly followed by the whole community, and celebrations after the game inevitably include singing and dancing.

Ceremonies are colourful, vibrant events which provide an endless display of traditional dance and dress. The Zulu monarchy hosts the annual Reed Dance and First Fruits Festival, and for the occasion the king's subjects arrive in their very best regalia. Magnificent beadwork in the form of belts, headdresses, necklaces and leg, arm and chest bands offset the use of skins, feathers and leatherwork embellished with chevrons and reflectors. The men carry sticks, shields and spears, while the women sometimes carry short decorative sticks or black umbrellas. White sneakers are favoured by both sexes as footwear, if any is worn.

Traditional Zulu dancing is very energetic and both men and women kick their legs and stamp their feet to the rhythm of skin-covered drums. Slight variations occur between regions and clans, but a general style is prevalent throughout. The men's dancing tends to show battle or hunting movements, during which they use their shields and sticks to great effect, while the women tend to dance more modestly and are not as regimental.

These complex steps and routines have been handed down through generations; perhaps the most interesting adaptation to modern circumstances is the introduction of certain restrictions of movement in a few of the male dances. In the past, many

35

36

Zulu men sought work on the mines and were obliged to stay in hostel accommodation. Living far from the rolling hills of KwaZulu-Natal, the men became homesick and, to ease their pain, they started dancing in the passageways of the hostels. In these narrow confines, the dancers were forced to restrict any wide movements and to direct them downwards and upwards. These modifications have endured and been retained in certain dances.

Unlike many African peoples, protracted initiation ceremonies marking the transition to adulthood do not occur among the Zulu. Courtship and betrothal rituals, in which strict protocol is observed and incestuous relationships forbidden, play an important role in the lives of young men and women.

A young man usually indicates his attraction for a girl while she is collecting water; she may have several admirers at the same time, but each will await his turn to express his love for her. It is customary for her, however, to pretend to ignore his advances and even his presence.

The girl's sisters and female peers are significantly involved in the courtship proceedings in that they form a support group or 'sisterhood' whose approval is essential if the young man is to make any headway in the courtship. He may find it necessary, for instance, to buy identical white sneakers or the same sweatshirt for each of the girls in order to smooth his way forward. Meanwhile the object of his affections feigns complete lack of interest and it may take many months of fast talking on his part before she makes her decision. Once she has made her choice of suitor (38), the girl sends members of her sisterhood to give him a necklace of white engagement beads, known as an *ucu*, to indicate her acceptance (37). The engaged man's family then raise a white flag at their homestead and the young man blows on a bull's horn or *telonka* to announce his engagement.

At the engagement ceremony, money is pinned onto the girl's hair net (35) by those who have come to join in the celebrations. As the girl and her sisterhood dance and sing in a long line (36), they plant spears into the ground at the feet of the men present. The men take turns to return the spears and perform an impromptu war dance or *ukugiya*, urged on by the guests. The engaged girl's future husband places a scarf, the fabric of which has been covered with pinned money, like a sash around the girl's shoulders to show to those present his high regard for her. She may paint a moustache on her lip and behave in other maverick ways, which is part of her period of defiance before she gets married.

For instance, at a marriage ceremony, the engaged girls blow whistles and dance exuberantly, making exhibitions of themselves with the approval of the community. During the

37

stick fighting they taunt and urge on the participants, blowing their whistles to add to the tension. After marriage a girl will undergo a complete change in her behaviour, showing deference to her husband and the other male members of his family as part of the practice of respect or *hlonipha*.

The Zulu practise Christianity in tandem with their belief in the ancestral spirits and their religious ceremonies reflect both the modern and the traditional. Zionist Christian churches are scattered throughout rural KwaZulu-Natal and can consist of little more than a shelter that has been set apart from the rest of the homestead. The 'Shembe' religious sect, in particular, use traditional dance and dress during ceremonies. The dancing and singing, accompanied by drums and trumpets, are stirring celebrations of their religious beliefs.

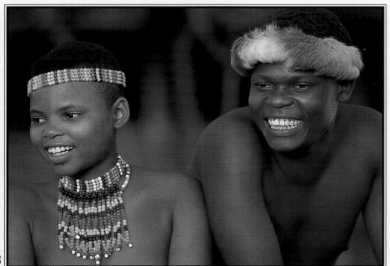

38

39

Weddings are traditionally large, unstructured gatherings with the actual ceremony starting around mid-afternoon. Throughout the day people arrive in a haphazard fashion to join in the festivities which take place on open ground near the bride-groom's homestead.

A wedding is not only a marriage between the bride and groom, but also an opportunity for the couple's families to air their grievances. Each family takes turns to dance and sing (39), during which time they publicly announce any indiscretions on the part of the other group. Censure against the bridegroom for making his daughter pregnant before the marriage, for example, will be raised by the bride's father, while at the same time praising the groom's other attributes. In this way any potential problems between the couple and their families are brought into the open and dealt with.

As with every Zulu ceremony, dancing, singing and beer drinking are an essential part of the proceedings. A combination of traditional dress and western style clothing helps to create a colourful affair. Gifts are exchanged between the young men and women from each group. These gifts, which may often be a comb, a necklace or a beaded belt, are returned to the owners at the end of the dance, the exchange being symbolic of the new ties between them.

The bride is dressed in an ox hide skirt, a collar made of animal skin and a structured headdress with a woollen veil covering her

40

41

42

face (40), which forms part of the practice of respect or *hlonipha*. Two feathers are placed in the band of her headdress representing the cattle her father has received as a bride wealth or *lobolo*. It is usual for a prospective husband to pay 11 cows to his future father-in-law, but, should his bride be pregnant or already have had children by him, he will be liable for additional cattle.

Older women who have mature children of their own, and therefore have a certain status in the community, behave outrageously on these occasions. They dance and ululate at will, often brandishing a small branch of a tree which symbolizes the spirit of the ancestors. Stick fighting is particularly popular at weddings and young men come from all over to compete against each other (41 and 42).

43

44

Zulu culture still places great emphasis on physical courage and fighting ability, and traditional weapons (47) remain an important part of a man's attire. Sticks, spears and shields are very important to the Zulu man who carries a shield and stick to most social gatherings and ceremonies, but especially to weddings where stick fighting is certain to take place. Even when out walking it would not be proper for a man to be seen without his sticks.

Shield and spear makers were, and still are, regarded as specialists in their field. Shields are made from ox hide which has been stretched out in the sun to dry before it is cut into the desired shape. Slits are then made down the centre and a strong smooth stick is threaded through the length of the shield as the handle. The slits are also decorative and occur on both the small ceremonial shield and the full body-sized shield which was designed to protect the warrior and conceal his weapons during Shakan times. Cow tails are tied to the top of the handle as added decoration and these are particularly effective while dancing when the dancer moves his shield around (44).

The small ceremonial shield is used during the traditional sport of stick fighting, a form of martial art greatly enjoyed by both young Zulu boys and men. The fighters carry the shield in one hand and a stick with an enlarged end in the other hand. The shield is used to ward off the opponent's blows which are aimed largely at the head of the fighter, although body blows are also counted. Contestants require agility and physical fitness to last the fight, as well as a good sense of humour as the blows often draw blood. Stick fighting presents an opportunity to settle old scores and, as opponents are required to shake hands after a bout, it has the effect of easing tensions between them.

45

46

Spears have long been used by the Zulu and primitive foundries in an open hearth with a rock anvil were used to forge spearheads. Today traditional spear makers are becoming increasingly rare, although they are still found in the remote rural areas (46). Great care is taken in the making of spearheads and blades, and, as the blades are considered purely utilitarian, no decorative finish is attempted. However, the shaft of the spear is sometimes decorated near the head.

Traditional male dress consists of two strips of hide hanging from a central waist band to which the tails of cows, monkeys or genets are added (45). Strips of rolled hide and/or beads may be worn across the chest or around the neck, and headdresses consist of a ring of hide, sometimes embellished with feathers and quills (48). The use of leopard skin signifies that the wearer is of royal blood – a chief or a chief's councillor (43). These days brightly coloured fabrics, bicycle chevrons and reflectors are added to the skins.

47

48

49

50

51

The Zulu believe in *Nkulunkulu*, a supreme being who created the earth but has little effect on their daily lives, which instead are guided by the ancestral spirits or *amadlozi*. Sacrifices are made to the *amadlozi* in order to appease them, but, should these not have a favourable effect, then a diviner or *sangoma* (53) is consulted in order to mediate with the spirits on the people's behalf.

Diviners are called to their profession by the ancestors and have special powers to communicate with them. They undergo an apprenticeship of approximately three years, during which time they are known as *amatwasa* (51). Diviners are consulted on matters of misfortune, illness and the future, and, because of their powers, they wield considerable influence in society. Their special status is borne out by their distinctive dress, and, although this may vary from area to area, the headdresses remain largely the same throughout. These are usually topped with the inflated bladders of sacrificed animals and the beads are strung in loops so that the spirits have somewhere to sit as they speak into their ears. As a symbol of their authority, diviners carry a fly whisk which is usually made from a wildebeest's tail (50).

Prior to talking with the ancestors, diviners burn a herb called *imphepho* and inhale the smoke to clear their heads, and a special infusion called *ubulawu* is whisked until it froths so as to help with divination. Seances, bone-throwing (49) and animal sacrifices are some of the methods used by *iZangoma* to help their patients. Traditional medicines or *muthi* are also prescribed in order to ward off evil spirits.

A diviner works in close association with the traditional healer or *inyanga* (52), who concocts herbal remedies for the treatment of illnesses. An assortment of barks, fruits, berries, leaves and roots are crushed or boiled to make medicines which are surprisingly effective, and are taken either by drinking, chewing or applying them to the skin.

In their western dress there is little to identify a *sangoma* or an *inyanga*, and quite often they occupy jobs in offices or other commercial enterprises. However, *iZangoma* will sometimes wear beaded headdresses and carry their fly whisks when dressed in western clothing.

The Zulu belief in the power of the ancestral spirits runs deep and, although today many Zulu live and work in the big cities of South Africa, this belief has not been eroded to any great extent. It is not uncommon for an urban Zulu to visit a *sangoma* or an *inyanga* for assistance, before consulting a western doctor.

52

53

54

55

Zulu people need little encouragement to break into song and dance. Wind instruments, such as flutes made from reeds, and string instruments, like the *makhweyana* (54), produce a gentle sound usually for the player's own pleasure.

Drums, built from tightly stretched cow hide (55), play an important role during dancing, the beat whipping the dancers into an energetic frenzy amid singing, clapping and whistling (56). Another popular musical instrument is the *ingungu* – a smooth stick attached to the hide on the inside of an open-ended drum. The stick is rubbed with wet fingers causing the hide to vibrate, giving rise to a sound similar to that made by a cello.

These days the guitar and accordion are skilfully played by the men which, to the accompaniment of Zulu lyrics, create an essentially African sound.

56